The Life and Adventures of Toby, the Sapient Pig

Cur*i*ous
PUBLICATIONS

Published by Curious Publications
101 W. 23rd St. #318
New York, NY 10011
curiouspublications.com

Copyright © 2021

Cover image: Wellcome Collection, from a colored etching by George Cruikshank, 1826
Frontispiece: John Leech, Public domain, via Wikimedia Commons
Toby broadside: Wikimedia Commons

Introductory text by Marc Hartzman.

ISBN-13: 978-1-7353201-5-1

Printed and bound in the United States of America.

A Brief Introduction

Those seeking inspiration or guidance often look to respected authors, philosophers, inventors, world leaders, and other famous people. But few, if any, look to a pig.

The swine race, however, should not be so easily discarded.

Toward the end of the eighteenth century, several learned porkers graced London theaters with their remarkable abilities. One of them, billed as "the amazing learned pig" was known to spell, do arithmetic, and tell time. His act was so popular he received top billing over human performers. As Ricky Jay reported in his 1986 book, *Learned Pigs & Fireproof Women*, a troupe of tightrope dancers and acrobats "were outraged at their second billing to a porcine pretender of prophecy." They made a stink about it to the theater's manager and demanded that either the pig go, or they would. "The troupe quickly sought new employment," Jay wrote.

However, a look back into the history of the species reminds us of its biggest shining star: Toby, the Sapient Pig.

Toby was a learned pig that achieved great fame in England in the early 1800s. Billed as "The only scholar of his race in the world," he, like learned pigs before him, could spell, read, play cards, tell time, perform blindfolded with twenty handkerchiefs over his eyes, and even guess people's ages.

An anecdote from an 1866 newspaper suggests the pig may have been responsible for the phrase "Mind your P's and Q's." The story, as it related, went as follows:

> When Toby, the learned pig, was in the zenith of his popularity, a theatrical wag, who attended the performance, maliciously set before him some peas, a temptation which the animal could not resist, and which immediately occasioned him to lose his *cue*. The pig exhibitor remonstrated with the author of the mischief on the unfairness of

what he had done, when he replied that his only wish was to see whether Toby knew his P's from his Q's.

Aside from Toby's mental acuity and fame, the skill which is of particular note at this very moment is his ability to write. With that glorious talent, he wrote the autobiography you now hold in your hand, *The Life and Adventures of Toby, the Sapient Pig; With His Opinions on Men and Manners*. Thus, his tale has been preserved through the centuries, allowing us all to marvel at his genius.

May Toby's words serve you well, whether you believe in writing pigs or not.

THE LIFE AND ADVENTURES

OF

TOBY,

THE SAPIENT PIG:

WITH HIS

Opinions on Men and Manners.

WRITTEN BY HIMSELF.

"ALL IMPOSTORS, WHEN THEY'RE KNOWN,
ARE PAST THEIR LABOUR AND UNDONE."

EMBELLISHED WITH AN ELEGANT FRONTISPIECE,
Descriptive of a
LITERARY PIG STY,
WITH THE AUTHOR IN DEEP STUDY.

LONDON:

PRINTED BY R. LYON, JOHN STREET, EDGWARE ROAD.
PUBLISHED AND SOLD BY NICHOLAS HOARE,
Proprietor and Teacher of Toby,
And may be had of all the Booksellers in the United Kingdom.
PRICE ONE SHILLING.

Entered at Stationers Hall.

DEDICATION

To the Nobility, Gentry, and the Public at large, who have witnessed my talents, and raised me from obscurity to the proud eminence on which I now stand, I dedicate my following *maiden* essay in literature.

As many great persons have before now become their own historians, I have thought proper to follow their example, not in the least doubting, that my literary labours will be rewarded with the same liberality as my performances have been, if they are entitled to the like meed of approbation.

I have been patronized by the first rank this *vast* empire has to boast of; to whom, as well as all my Patrons and Friends, I beg leave to return my most ardent thanks; and, while I breathe, (possessed of my mental powers, which from my *youth*, and lack of experience, are but *now* in the *bud*,) I will on every occasion, that calls them into action, shew an earnest intention to render them *effective*, and *impressive*, from an *active* display of their *native* energies. In me the world will see, and posterity may read, a lesson in my existence and labours, that *time, assiduity*, and *patience*, led on by perseverance, will ultimately surmount every obstacle (though as high as the pinnacles of *Agra*) which may retard the progress of *genius*.

TOBY,
The Sapient Pig.

PREFACE

It must undoubtedly be acknowledged by the most *fastidious* critic, that, a production from a being like *me*, must be a work of *originality*; or, at least, in the character of an *author*, I must be so, being the first of my *race* that ever wielded the pen. I there fore fear not their lash;—besides, it would be derogatory to those *vast* pre-eminent *self* created mortals, to touch me at all. Secure in my *own* insignificance, I feel happy; and, shall take the liberty of adding one more name to the list of authors (by far too numerous for what they are good for) with which the world has been furnished.

T. S. P.

THE
LIFE AND ADVENTURES
OF
TOBY,
The Sapient Pig.

I was born in a place, if I am rightly informed, called *Aversall*, or *Aversham*, on the *Duke of Bedford's* demesnes. My *father* was an *independent gentleman*, who roamed at large over his Grace's lands; and my *Mother* a *spinster*, in the service of a person whose name I have forgot (he kept an inn, or road-side house, called the *Green Man*, at the above mentioned place;) she was of a prolific nature, and I was one, among many more, who were the offsprings of an *illicit amour* between her

*But no fool's day with me.

and my father. On my natal day, the first of April, 1816,* (nearly about the precise time I drew my first breath) the gentleman, who has since been my friend and preceptor, and to whom I owe every comfort I now enjoy, from the great care he has all along taken in the cultivation of my mind and manners, was travelling that road. The above sign attracted his notice, under which was written the following words:

"You may go further and fare worse."

Being somewhat fatigued, he took the advice, and entered accordingly. At that moment an elderly man came in at the back door of the house, which, by the bye, was no other than my mother's master, rubbing his hands, highly pleased at the event, he exclaimed "Dame! Bess," (for that was my mother's name), "is farrowing." The good old woman, nay, the whole house, was in a bustle at the news; and all, with the before mentioned gentleman, hastened *(sans ceremonie)* to the place of her *accouchement*, which was in an outhouse hard by, just as I came forth—they all instantly expressed their admiration of me; and on their return to the house it was agreed between the gentleman and my mother's master, that I should, for a small gratuity, immediately become the property of the former; or, at least, let me be rightly understood, that as he had taken a liking to me, I should be placed under his care; my mother having so large a family, and her master anxious to get them off her hands as soon as possible that he might sooner reap the benefit of her service in the same kind of way: for he never heeded her profligacy, so long as it was instrumental in feeding his avarice. Alas! to gratify his ruling passion, the dearest it was of all "Nature's ties," (the separation of an affectionate mother from her tender babe at so early a period) "were torn asunder."

The gentleman, after refreshing himself, put me in a little box, which he purchased for that purpose; and placing me under his arm, sallied forth, much pleased at having me, though at that time I was scarce three quarters of an hour old, from that he presaged, having never sucked my mother, I had not imbibed the temper of my progenitors, (except in the instance of my birth,) which, I am told, was not of a pleasant nature, but, on the contrary, the most obstinate on record; and as I have never since been suffered to mix with any of the family, being so closely confined to my studies, and the advice that my kind master and benefactor has repeatedly given me, never to do so on any account, determined me to be firm in that resolve. Indeed, were it not for the strong re semblance I bear to them, the world, from the knowledge it has of my extraordinary talents, would conceive me to be a person of another description entirely.

From the moment I left the place of my nativity, my preceptor became my constant companion by day and by night; asleep or awake he was but few removes from me. I wish all Tutors would discharge their duties in the like manner; if they did, we should not have so many block heads in the world as we see every day: and truly they are a very numerous race.

As it was a matter of chance, for some time, whether my master and I succeeded or not, in point of talent, he doubted much; recollecting *Hamlet's* soliloquy, "TO BE, OR NOT TO BE," he involuntarily used those words in addressing me. The idea was such, that it determined him as to my name; and hence was derived its origin.

From his bringing me up by hand in the way he did, and having no one to associate with but himself, I imbibed an affection for him, that will end only with my last breath; and it is a source, if not the principal one, of my taking his precepts so readily, and knowing what they meant, as it were, by instinct, without fear of chastisement, for he never thrashed me but once, and I have remembered it ever since. Whenever he set about giving me a lesson, day or night were alike to him in so doing; watching every movement of my mind with a solicitude indescribable, and a promptness of application, never equalled by any of the learned teachers at either of our Universities.

Such a constant pursuit worked the happiest effects on my mind; he soon, much to his satisfaction, began to see its emanations; and when they were in full force, his precepts were so admirably given, that, wonderful to relate, before I was three months old, I knew some of my letters; this was such a discovery to him, that he redoubled his attentions, and then began to conceive he would one day make a great creature of me; which the world has manifested, the world has acknowledged, and the world is every day rewarding, with its usual liberality, his genius, industry, patience and perseverance.

By the time I was four months old, I could read tolerably well: at present I know many little boys and girls, at four years old, that can not do any thing like it. What a shame that will appear to them, and how angry will they be with themselves, when they are able to read this my life, that one of my race should so far surpass them at so tender an age.

As we proceeded, my master was astonished at the capaciousness of my mind, and he relaxed somewhat of his former assiduity, which made me a little angry with him; he smiled, but has since told me, it arose from the best of intentions, being fearful that he might nip in the bud that which one day would bloom, and become the rarest flower in creation.

When his lessons were over, he always left me to myself, (having no companion.) A perfect recluse, I was without amusement, except ruminating on what I had seen and heard; by which means, they were ever in my "mind's eye," and became so impressed on it, that I was anxious, nay eager, to learn more and more; for as my stock of learning encreased, I felt vain, and took a still greater delight in increasing it.

My master, though tender, I used at times to

think severe; for he would keep me so sparingly, and especially before school hours; yet I must do him the justice to say I never went hungry to bed, as many little ladies and gentlemen do very often. More shame for them! for nothing, I think, can be so bad as to be unruly, or obstinately bent on not paying attention to the wishes of an indulgent parent, whose sole anxiety is for their happiness, and who frequently do many injuries to others to be able to discharge their duty towards them: The fostering hand of a parent is a blessing I never knew, and I often lament it; but providence is all sufficient, and will never desert those whose actions entitle them to its care.

In this way we went on from day to day, myself improving every lesson, and my master more zealously studious than ever to my interest. As I improved in mind, so I did in person, which was now likewise beginning to shew itself. A circumstance that gave him no little pleasure, convinced of the additional attraction it would ensure me.

During the time, from the first moment he had me till now, nothing had given him the least alarm respecting my welfare, as I was very healthy and promising; but about that period an event happened that had like to have dashed the cup (of which he was desirous of tasting) from his lips for ever.

Here I must give my reader to understand, that my master was owner and manager of an equestrian troop of some eminence, that travelled the country; amongst his stud of horses, which I have been told was an excellent one, was a very spirited animal, whom they generally (to keep down his vicious spirit) worked the hardest; and for that purpose he always drew the truck on which some of the company rode when we travelled from one town to another. My master in his gig, and myself in a kind of boot, or box, that he had fixed behind it, for the purpose of carrying me easy, and unperceived by the people on the road, always led the cavalcade; one day, as we were passing a narrow lane, on one side of which was a ditch, the horse before mentioned took fright at a man, who suddenly popped through the hedge, and set off at full speed. The endeavours of his driver to stop him was of no avail; and in dashing by us, he caught our off wheel, and precipitated my master, self, and chaise, into the ditch, with a tremendous crash. As soon as he had recovered himself, the first thing he sought after was my safety; for he expected nothing but

pecuniary way we heeded not, but kept performing, though to

"A beggarly account of empty boxes."

In the hopes the period would soon arrive when I, like many others that have gone before me, might be taken by the hand-patronized, and ushered into public notice, under the auspices of some distinguished character, and my fame and fortune stamped for ever, we bore our misfortunes like christians; but I shall never forget the privations we endured.

The life of an itinerant player abounds with more variety than any other; to give even a faint sketch of ours, would far exceed my limits. There is an old saying, *"when things come to the worst they mend."* And with us it was fully verified; for if it had not been, that my improvement in the *histrionic* art was every day more and more apparent, we should have given it up altogether, so greatly at times were we dismayed.

The period at last arrived when we were to be solaced for all our sufferings; and an agreement was entered into with the proprietor of the *"Royal Promenade Rooms,"* Spring Gardens for my first appearance before a London audi-

entitled to the protection of society, as the most exalted personage in existence.

With feelings like these, I amply revenged myself in an encounter we had with each other, which brought him a little to his senses. It was the first time I had ever seen a man drunk. My master, I believe, being one of the soberest men alive. As our immortal poet says,

"Oh! that a man should put an enemy in his mouth to steal away his brains."

From that moment I became disgusted with inebriety, and hope I shall always be so. If a man did but know how far he lessens his dignity, and how near he approaches, nay outsteps the brute creation, in his thoughts, words, and deeds, besides the offence he offers to the sober eye, at the blush of modesty, he would never again be found in that degraded state.

It was my master's determination to accustom me as much as possible to the sight of the public under whatever disadvantage might present it self; and to speak truth, for a length of time, during the winter of last year, and the beginning of the spring of the present, they were numberless. Though we were not rewarded in a

he deemed it fit that I should make my first bow to an audience, that he had drawn together in a poor village in Essex: it consisted chiefly of labouring men.

Though before an indifferent tribunal, his hopes and fears were all alive; and never did I see a man so agitated as he was during that my first entrance on the boards. My success was beyond every idea he could have formed on it; and so well pleased was he, that, ere I went to rest, he rewarded me accordingly.

About the middle of my performance, a young farmer came in, whom I did not at first sight approve of, there appearing to me something about him which I had never before seen. For, till that evening, I had never known any thing of the world, and therefore was at a loss to know what was the matter with him; but he soon taught me to know, for his conduct was so different from the rest. He insulted every body, more or less; among others, myself—at which I took an offence; for I had been taught to know, that though I had embarked in a profession, that by some is deemed not the most respectable, yet every person, let his situation in life be what it may, whose conduct is irreproachable, is as much

my total destruction; however, to his inexpressible joy, found me as usual, except a little stupid, occasioned by a slight contusion I had received on the side of the head from the accident.

If he had been deprived of me, I really think he never would have held up his head any more, so great were his expectations of me; and particularly so, when I inform you, that he had tried twelve of my species before, but had never, after infinite pains, trouble, and expence, been able to promise himself ultimate success: consequently dropped each fruitless pursuit.

Every thing being righted, we sat off again, and he soon learnt, to his satisfaction, that the animal had been stopt without doing any further injury. From this time, I knew not the reason but the affairs of my master every day grew worse and worse; one misfortune or another attended him constantly, they bore him down: and he became at last quite indifferent to any thing but me.

Those who were about him, and to whom in many instances he had been a friend, took advantage of it; and so, by quick, but imperceptible degrees, hastened his downfall. Finding his affairs irretrievable, he sat about perfecting my education; and by the time I was six months old,

ence. The celebrity I had attained in the country had somewhat run before me in the way of newspaper report; but when I was formally announced to perform, I became the topic of the day—expectation was on the wing—the prying eye of curiosity was wide open—and the most arduous task I should ever have to accomplish, was now before me. Those who have been in a similar situation, can alone be able to conceive what I must have felt: as the time grew nearer, it was dreadful; however, I possess a strong nerve, and some small share of confidence, which, I was convinced, would greatly assist me, and in the trial I found them adequate to my purposes. The day arrived that was to *make* me or *mar* me for ever; the house was crowded at an early hour by persons of the first rank and fashion such an assemblage of beauty I had never before witnessed. My first appearance was greeted with loud and reiterated plaudits; from every part handkerchiefs waving—fans rapping—placards exhibited;—in fact, the tumults of applause were greater than ever was known before.

The encouragement such a flattering reception afforded, roused every latent spark of genius in me; and the brilliancy of my mind shone like a constellation. As I proceeded through the various scenes I had to depict, I received every testimony of approbation I could wish; and the close of my scenic effort was crowned with universal applause.

Never, till then, was my heart so elated: my master was mute in astonishment at the success of my onset; and we consoled each other, when all was over, at the golden harvest that presented itself.

The next morning the papers teemed with critiques on my performance all were liberal in the end (for a good reason, because I had the Town on my side;) but they twisted me sadly some of the editors, from what they wrote, I firmly believe had never been there. In one of the papers I read the following from an unknown hand:

TOBY,

The Sapient Pig;

OR THE THREE GREAT ACTORS.

A New Song to an Old Tune.

Of all that the world ever yet brought to light,
The most wonderful is, Sirs, the subject I write;
Pythagoreans now are all bound to maintain
Their Philosopher's right, as Toby proves plain.
                Derry down, &c.

The mania for actors is now all the rage,
And therefore my actor is brought on the stage;
For though he's not swallow'd *Will Shakespear* quite,
Yet on his *own* text he can throw a *new* light.
                Derry down, &c.

The favourite of *Drury* they reckon so *Kean*,
He's so cutting at times they weep with both e'en,
And then at the Garden they've got a new Booth,
But so small, and so trifling, they all say forsooth,
                Derry down, &c.

His grunt Catalanian notes far surpasses,
And then he's so learned in all learning's classes,
That Lawyers, and Proctors, and Statesmen allow,
At the bar, or in senate, he'll laurel his brow.
                Derry down, &c.

Then which of these rivals, amidst their range of parts,
Who from nature, for a moment never departs;

Why the *Public* at large, will with *Critics* agree,
That our *Sapient* Pig *Toby's* the best of the Three.
> Derry down, &c.

How proud *Uncle Toby* will be when he knows,
With success his namesake the two does oppose:
To learn the *Moot* case, when the news is sent down,
He'll order friend Corporal Trim up to town.
> Derry down &c.

Then all who with wonder would wish to surprize,
Their senses, and feelings, and marvel their eyes,
No longer loose time, as it is now all the gig,
But go and see Toby, the rare Sapient Pig.
> Derry down, &c.

The foregoing was sung in the streets, my picture was sold in the shops, though I never sat for my likeness; every person of talent was forthcoming with something about me; anecdote, after anecdote. Among the rest, was one, whether true or not, I cannot say, but it bears with it some apparent reason.

My mother, in the early stage of her pregnancy, unwittingly entered a gentleman's flower garden; where, after amusing herself with culling each simple, and traversing its spacious rounds, she came obliquely to the entrance of his library, it had glass folding doors, even with the floor; one of them being on the jar, she entered, and in a short time cast her eye over the numerous volumes it contained; such was her haste, she disordered the whole classical arrangement, slightly passing over some, while others she minutely perused, nay absolutely bereived of their leaves, chewing and swallowing them, so great was her avidity.

This was told to account for my uncommon talents; but I leave the public to judge of its truth, not willing to draw any conclusions on that head myself.

I now had the honor to be sent for to the stately mansions of persons of the first rank, to give select performances, and there I

"Out Herod, Herod."

This was a source of additional wealth and fame; such never attended me before; when a person's name is up, it is every thing. The carriage in which I rode drew up to their doors, and mixed with the rest, as if its owner was equal to any of them. In fact, the *whips* crowded round *mine*, anxious to know how and when he came into my service; and to learn every thing concerning so popular a character as myself.

I have read of philosophers whose abstemiousness was held forth as patterns of sobriety, but none ever exceeded mine, for since I was six weeks old I have never tasted any thing but bread and water hence arises my purity.

A gentleman who one evening witnessed my performances, was so struck with it that he wrote as follows.

Toby, the Sapient Pig.

Whether heaven to brutes has imparted a mind
Is a quere that moralists have not defin'd;
Perhaps it may rather arise from their pride,
Than their reason, that reason to brutes they've denied.
Those, at least, who the *Sapient Toby* have seen,
To the latter opinion decidedly lean.
His symptoms of sense, deep astonishment raise,
And elicit applauses of wonder and praise.
What a theme for his muse here the poet may find,
What a scope is here given the contemplative mind,
What a parallel may the philosopher pen,
'Twixt the *nature* of brutes, and the *reason* of men!
But scarce can a doubt any longer remain,

Toby, the Sapient Pig

The reason that Toby displays is so plain;
Here wisdom itself greater wisdom may find,
And no longer be vain of the *rational* mind,
Since Toby approaches to reason so nigh,
She may bid all her boasted self consequence fly;
And folly may stoop by a pig to be taught,
The value of sense and the richness of thought
Here the learned may see what pains and what art,
Have been ta'en to make *Toby* so well play his part;
How with patience his Master must have been endued,
E'er the temper of *Toby* was wholly subdued;
And what praise there is due to the *mortal* whose power
Makes a *Pig spell* and *read*, or e'en *tell* you *the hour*.
Here the silken rob'd peer and the delicate belle,
Are unsullied by filth, unoffended by smell;
Toby turns all disdainful from deeds of offence,
For what would so blast i pretensions to sense?
Of the crowds who the *Sapient Toby* have seen,
Not one of them all disappointed have been;
But all to their friends have been proud to repeat,
That a *Visit* to *Toby* indeed is a treat.

Φίλων Σοφος.

To the Public I shall ever be grateful; and I hope the foregoing, which is literally the truth, may meet with their approbation.

THE END.

Printed by H. Lyon, John Street, Edgeware Road.

TOBY

THE
SAPIENT PIG,

From the Royal Rooms, Spring Gardens,

The only Scholar of his Race in the World.

THIS MOST EXTRAORDINARY CREATURE
Will Spell and Read, Cast Accounts,
PLAY AT CARDS;
Tell any Person what o'Clock it is to a Minute
BY THEIR OWN WATCH,
ALSO TELL THE AGE OF ANY ONE IN COMPANY,

And what is more Astonishing he will
Discover a Person's Thoughts
A Performance beyond all others the most Incredible.

Mr. HOARE having spent a number of Years in accomplishing this great undertaking, leaves it to a discerning Public, to judge of the laborious task he has had in bringing the above Animal before them, as of all others in Nature, none are so obstinate as his species, and it is only by unremitted assiduity and attention, that he has finally brought to such great perfection what Man never did before.
He is in Colour the most beautiful of his Race, in Symmetry the most Perfect, in Temper the most Docile; his Nature is so far from being offensive, that he is pleasing to all who honor him with their presence.

The silken sob'd peer, and the delicate belle,
Are unsullied by filth, uncoffended by smell;
Toby turns all disdainful from deeds of offence,
For what would so blast his pretensions to sense.

He EXHIBITS every day at the
Temple Rooms, Fleet-street,
Near TEMPLE BAR, opposite CHANCERY LANE,

At the Hours of 1 and 3, precisely,
And again in the Evening at 7 and 9 o'Clock.
ADMITTANCE ONE SHILLING.

Just Published, The Life & Adventures of TOBY the SAPIENT PIG,
With his Opinion on Men and Manners,
May be had at the Exhibition Rooms, Price One Shilling.

Printed by H. LYON, John Street, Edgware Road.

ALSO FROM
CURIOUS PUBLICATIONS

The Embalmed Head of Oliver Cromwell: A Memoir
by Marc Hartzman

Psycho-Phone Messages
by Francis Grierson

Spectropia, or Surprising Spectral Illusions Showing Ghosts Everywhere
by J. H. Brown

Spirit Slate Writing and Kindred Phenomena
by William E. Robinson

The Sight of Hell
by Rev. John Furniss

How to Speak With the Dead: A Practical Handbook
by Sciens

The Talking Dead: A Collection of Messages from Beyond the Veil, 1850s-1920s
Edited by Marc Hartzman

Reminiscences of the Elephant Man
by Sir Frederick Treves and Others

Vampires and Vampirism
by Dudley Wright

curiouspublications.com

www.ingramcontent.com/pod-product-compliance
Lightning Source LLC
Chambersburg PA
CBHW020303030426
42336CB00010B/895